The Murder
of
Christina Collins

**The story of the 'Bloody Steps' murder of 1839 on the
Trent & Mersey Canal that inspired the award
winning Inspector Morse novel**
The Wench is Dead

John Godwin
& Antony J. Richards

with an introduction by
Colin Dexter

First published in 2011 by
The Irregular Special Press
for Baker Street Studios Ltd
Endeavour House
170 Woodland Road, Sawston
Cambridge, CB22 3DX, UK

Setting © Baker Street Studios Ltd, 2011
Introduction © Colin Dexter, 2010
Main Text © John Godwin, 1990
Gazetteer © Antony J. Richards, 2011

ISBN: 1-901091-44-9 (10 digit)
ISBN: 978-1-901091-44-1 (13 digit)

Cover Concept: Antony J. Richards

John Godwin is indebted to the following persons: Mrs. Joan Anslow for the sketches of
George Smith and William Calcraft, the William Salt Library of Stafford for access to old
copies of the *Staffordshire Gazette*, Professor Edwin A. Dawes of Hull University for
permission to use illustrations from his collection along with additional valued help, my wife
for typing and checking the original script, and my son Phillip for help in the production of the
original booklet.

Typeset in 8/14pt Times New Roman

CONTENTS

INTRODUCTION 5
FROM LACE TO MAGIC 7
FROM LIVERPOOL TO RUGELEY 11
THE VERDICT 23
CHRISTINA'S LEGACY 35
GAZETTEER 39
    ASTON LOCK 39
    BODLEIAN LIBRARY (OXFORD) 39
    BRINDLEY BANK (RUGELEY) 39
    CASTLE INN (WOLVERHAMPTION) 40
    COLWICH LOCK 40
    COVENTRY CANAL 40
    CROSSHALL STREET (LIVERPOOL) 41
    EDGWARE ROAD (LONDON) 41
    FAZELEY 42
    FRADLEY JUNCTION 42
    HARECASTLE TUNNEL 42
    HOO MILL LOCK 44
    LYCEUM THEATRE (LONDON) 44
    NEW RADFORD (NOTTINGHAMSHIRE) 44
    NOTTINGHAM JOURNAL 45
    OXFORD CANAL 45
    PICKFORDS COMPANY 46
    PRESTON BROOK 47
    RUGELEY 48
    SAINT AUGUSTINE'S CHURCH (RUGELEY) 49
    SANDON LOCK 50
    SHOULDER OF MUTTON INN (RUGELEY) 50
    STAFFORD 50
    STAFFORD ASSIZES 51
    STAFFORD COUNTY GAOL 52
    STAFFORDSHIRE GAZETTE 55
    STOKE-ON-TRENT 55
    STONE 56
    TALBOT INN (RUGELEY) 56
    TRENT & MERSEY CANAL 57
    WILLIAM SALT LIBRARY (STAFFORD) 58
    WOOD END LOCK 59

[Colin Dexter, the creator of Inspector Morse, standing on the
infamous 'Bloody Steps' at RUGELEY]

INTRODUCTION

When the slim, buff-coloured envelope dropped through the letter-box, I could never have had the slightest idea that it contained a booklet that would dominate my thinking for many days, many days and many hours: *The Murder of Christina Collins*, subtitled The 'Bloody Steps' Murder. How on earth could it have occurred to me that fairly soon I should be standing and photographed, if not on the original, but at least on the present flight of those self-same 'Bloody Steps'.

The booklet had been given to me by Harry Judge, a distinguished educationalist, who lives, like me, in what John Thaw always called 'leafy North Oxford'. The story concerns the death of a sprightly, attractive, clever, well-educated, thirty-seven-year-old woman, most barbarously treated and drowned in the TRENT & MERSEY CANAL at RUGELEY in 1839, by a group of callous, illiterate, drunken boatmen. That is what we find in the judicial records. That is what we read on Christina's gravestone. Three boatmen were arrested for this wicked deed; two were publicly hanged; one was deported to Australia; and one, a youngish lad, not prosecuted. Little more to the story, really.

Or was there, perhaps ...?

Research has hitherto played only a minimal part in my writings of detective tales – but not so now. I took a trip on a 'narrow boat' to familiarise myself with life on the OXFORD CANAL; I made two journeys to talk with John Godwin, the author of the booklet; I spent two days at the WILLIAM SALT LIBRARY in STAFFORD, reading through the contemporary reporting of the murder, and the subsequent trial, in the *STAFFORDSHIRE GAZETTE*; and in the BODLEIAN LIBRARY I consulted a copy of *Emperor of Conjurors'* by Thomas Ingleby, Christina's first husband. And such research was not only of considerable interest to me, but also most opportune, since at about that time I had been thinking of writing another case to be solved by Inspector Morse in which there were no further clues whatsoever on which to exercise his eccentric imagination. Was this murder such a case? It surely ought to be, perhaps, after a hundred and fifty years ... or were there a few aspects of the tantalising story that suggested the possibility of some fictional re-working of the whole grizzly affair?

At this time, recollections of a recent fortnight's hospitalisation were much in mind for me, and I decided to stick Morse in the John Radcliffe Hospital in Oxford, and have one of his friends visiting him with a copy of the same booklet, I fictionalised the whole thing, moving events about forty years later than the 1830s, setting the discovery of the body in the OXFORD CANAL, (of course!), and with wholly new names and relationships for the main characters. The outcome of all this was the publication in 1989 of *The Wench is Dead,* a novel which in that year won

5

the Gold Dagger from the Crime Writers' Association. Not that the novel was free of faults! Writing about the past is like treading through a minefield, and I received much correspondence on my sad ignorance of female underclothing in the nineteenth century, and about the dating of the transportation of criminals to Australia. But what remained in my own mind was the pretty firm conviction that the verdict of 'guilty' pronounced upon the boatmen would, if challenged in the courts today, be considered 'unsafe'. Evidence for the murder was completely circumstantial. And who could be produced who had witnessed any sign of criminal behaviour at or near the scene of the 'murder'? No one. I have never maintained that the original verdict amounted to a miscarriage of justice. How could I? But I have changed things a little? Yes. In fact I have changed things a lot …

Read on!

Colin Dexter

FROM LACE TO MAGIC

[The gravestone of Christina Collins at SAINT AUGUSTINE'S CHURCH in RUGELEY]

A few years ago, most of the tombstones in the churchyard of RUGELEY parish church were removed from their sites to facilitate the maintenance of the grassed area around the church. A few headstones that had particular local interest were left in place. One of these, on the south side of the church, bears an epitaph that is still decipherable, though the stone is beginning to crumble. It reads as follows:

> *To the memory of Christina Collins, the wife of Robert Collins,*
> *London, who having been most barbarously treated was found dead*
> *in the canal in this Parish on June 17th 1839, aged 37 years. This*
> *stone is erected by some individuals of the Parish of Rugeley in*
> *commiseration of the end of this unhappy woman.*

Behind this simple, yet poignant, statement lies the story of drunken lust and lechery, and of a helpless woman at the mercy of coarse and brutal boatmen during the nightmare canal journey over a hundred and seventy years ago.

Christina (christened Christiana) was born on 17th July 1801 in NEW RADFORD, Nottingham. Her father, Robert Brown, had made several inventions connected with the Nottingham lace industry, and had patented some of these. Patent No. 2766 dated 1804 was for 'a machine to be affixed or attached to horizontal, warp or Vandyke knitting frames for the purpose of manufacturing by a more simple, neat and expeditious method, lace or network of various figures and qualities, with thread, silk, cotton, worsted or other material produced from animal, vegetable or mineral fibres'. Two years earlier, he had taken out patent No. 2571 for 'the invention of a machine for the purpose of manufacturing by this more speedy, simple or neat method, fishing nets, horse nets, garden nets, furniture nets, nets for wearing apparel, and all other articles of net work … and also for manufacturing divers other figured meshes, with any thread, twist, twine, cord, jersey or yarn produced from animal or mineral substances'.

Mr. Brown apparently did not prosper from his inventions for as long as he might have hoped. He was a man of undoubted ingenuity, but it seems that the prosecution of his inventions swallowed up his resources. Later the family fell on hard times. Before he died in 1818 Mr. Brown was receiving Parish Relief. Towards the end of his life he became mentally deranged and attempted suicide. One of his sons, Alfred (Christina's brother) made an effort to exploit his father's inventions further, but he was only a small newsvendor, and although an intelligent man, he lacked finance and did not succeed. Christina had been well educated, and does not appear to have taken easily to the reduced circumstances of the family. One local newspaper, commenting on Christina's background reported after her death that she had been 'well formed to move in a different sphere, but the unforeseen events which occurred in Mr. Brown's family, when the children were young, blighted all their prospects, and left them without friends or protectors to guide them in the rugged paths of existence'. After Mr. Brown's death, Christina's mother was forced to go out to work to make ends meet, and she was in fact employed in nursing until well after her sixtieth birthday. Mrs. Brown was not told of her daughter's murder for some time after the event, for fear of upsetting her unduly. When the news was eventually broken to her, the *NOTTINGHAM JOURNAL* commented, 'Her distress at the untimely death of her daughter is extreme. It has revived remembrances of earlier years, and days of prosperity, when friends smile, and her prospects promised much happiness. She is much respected among the families that have employed her, and we are told is very grateful for acts of kindness'.

Christina's first husband was Thomas Ingleby, a Scotsman from Dundee. He was a conjurer by profession, and appeared in London and provincial theatres. In order to attract publicity he assumed the title of

'Emperor of all the Conjurors', but when he found that a rival had assumed the same title, he had the following statement on all the theatre handbills, underneath his name: 'Mr. Ingleby, the greatest man in the world, most respectfully informs the Nobility, Gentry and Public in general that, in consequence of his superior excellence in the Art of Deception, he has had conferred upon him, in the last week, the title of Emperor of all Conjurors by a numerous assemblage of Gentleman Amateurs; and particularly through the amazing trick of cutting a fowl's head off and restoring it to life and animation, for no man knows the real way but himself'.

Ingleby had made his first appearance in London at the LYCEUM THEATRE in 1807. The trick, on which he prided himself was really very simple. Two similar cockerels were chosen, and one concealed while the other had its head cut off in front of the audience. While the head was being examined by the audience, the concealed cockerel, with its head tucked under its wing, was substituted for the decapitated one. When the head was returned to the conjuror, he spoke a few magic words and slipped the head of the living bird from under its wing. The cockerel then struggled to its feet. Another trick of Ingleby's was to boil a fowl for twenty minutes in front of the audience, then appear to take it out of the water, while uttering a few magic words. The fowl (another one, of course) ran around the stage a few times, to the delight of the audience.

Ingleby toured the provinces quite extensively, and he appeared in the Assembly Room of the CASTLE INN, Wolverhampton, for five consecutive nights in April 1822. By this time he had enlarged his repertoire considerably. It now included a trick whereby he allowed a spectator 'to take away the life of any animal under the size of a calf' and then, 'by one blast of his magic breath to restore it to life again'. In another of his tricks, he offered to break a gentleman's watch into twenty pieces and then to return it to its owner 'as good as when first presented'. For his final act, Ingleby 'if bespoke the day before, as he must not eat any dinner on that day' would eat half a dozen knives and forks!

Prices of admission to Ingleby's show were two shillings (10p) for front seats, and one shilling (5p) for back seats. In the later years of his performances, Christina – who often referred to her theatrical connections – became a part of Ingleby's performance. At first she contributed recitations and songs to the repertoire. Later her items were more ambitious, and handbills stated she would 'honour herself by performing the extravaganza of the invisible hen'. Towards the end of Ingleby's life, she had added dancing to her acts.

[Inside cover of Ingleby's *The Whole Art of Legerdemain*]

Ingleby – who was some years older than Christina – wrote a book about conjuring in 1815, entitled *The Whole Art of Legerdemain*. It is now a collector's item. In Frost's book, *Lives of the Conjurors* it states that Ingleby died in the summer of 1832 at Enniscorthy, 'a small town in Ireland'. Frost deduces that Ingleby was 'less fortunate, or less provident than most of the conjuring fraternity, and continued his professional wanderings until his death'. Frost also mentions that he left a young widow, but no children are mentioned. This confirms what is known from other sources, namely that Ingleby died childless.

FROM LIVERPOOL TO RUGELEY

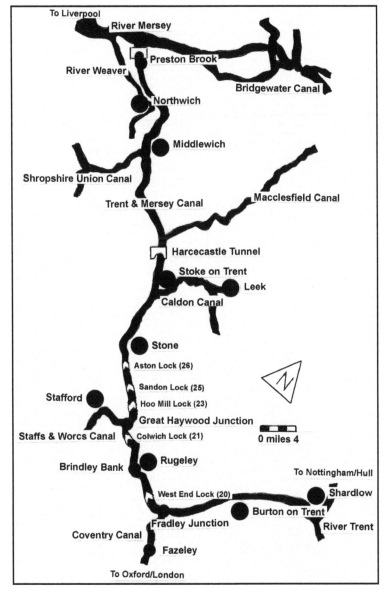

[The route of Christina Collins along the
TRENT & MERSEY CANAL]

11

One may reasonably suppose that the reduced social status Christina had endured since the collapse of her father's wealth had resulted in her marrying the itinerant conjuror. Her next husband was also of low social status, though there is no doubt whatever of Christina's love for him. Some time after Ingleby's death she met Robert Collins, an ostler.

[No. 3 CROSSHALL STREET, Liverpool, where Christina worked]

They married in 1838, and went to Liverpool to find work, but this was not easy, as times were very hard. Christina found employment as a seamstress at the house of a Mrs. Grice, at No. 3 CROSSHALL STREET, but by the end of May 1839, Robert, still unsuccessful in his quest for work, decided to try his luck in London. Here he secured employment as an ostler, and found lodgings at No. 10 EDGWARE ROAD. On June 8th he sent his wife a guinea (105p) – all he could afford – and asked her to join him in London as soon as possible. It seems that he had missed his wife dreadfully, and in a letter that Christina wrote to her husband at this time, she refers to the mental state through which he was passing in London. 'My dear Collins', she began (she always referred to him by his surname), 'Sorry I am to read your wandering letter to me. Do my dear strive against that misfortune which I fear awaits you. The loss of reason is dreadful'.

[Today the marina at PRESTON BROOK is still busy]

On the morning of Saturday 15th June 1839 Christina, carrying two small trunks, bade Mrs. Grice farewell, and made her way by barge from Liverpool to PRESTON BROOK at the northern terminus of the TRENT & MERSEY CANAL, that had been opened sixty two years earlier. Here she joined a PICKFORDS COMPANY boat that was departing for STOKE-ON-TRENT, RUGELEY, FRADLEY JUNCTION, and thence via the COVENTRY CANAL and OXFORD CANAL systems to London. The fare was sixteen shillings (80p); much cheaper than the fare by the newly opened railway line from Liverpool to London.

Christina was a petite and attractive figure wearing a dark coloured gown with a fawn coloured handkerchief over her neck, and a figured blue silk bonnet with a light ribbon. The clothes were not new, but she had a very tidy appearance.

The captain of the boat was James Owen from Brinklow, near Coventry. He was a bluff type of man, married and aged thirty-nine. The members of the crew were twenty-seven-year-old George Thomas, alias Dobell, a single man who had left his home at Wombourne, Staffordshire eleven years earlier; William Ellis, alias Lambert, the twenty-eight-year-old illiterate son of a labourer from Brinklow; and a teenager, William Musson, from Chilvers Coton, Warwickshire. The boat left PRESTON BROOK at 7.30 p.m. on Saturday 15th June, and Christina's dead body was found in the canal at BRINDLEY BANK, near the aqueduct, about a mile from the town, at 5.00 a.m. on Monday 17th June.

After a coroner's inquest at the TALBOT INN, RUGELEY, the three boatmen were charged with her murder and were committed to STAFFORD COUNTY GOAL. In the trial held at the STAFFORDSHIRE ASSIZES in July 1839 there were four indictments against the men – wilful murder of Christina Collins by throwing her into the canal; rape upon her (with different counts charging different prisoners with being principals in commission of the offence and the others as aiders and abettors); common assault; and stealing articles, the property of her husband. Musson, the boy, who was originally charged with them, was not named in the indictment.

Mr. Sergeant Ludlow, for the prosecution, said he should first proceed on the charge of rape. However, after the completion of his case, the judge (Mr. Justice Williams) decided that there was no proof of the prisoners having committed the crime, and the jury, under his direction, found a verdict of not guilty. Mr. Sergeant Ludlow then applied to the court to put off the trial under the indictment for murder until the next assizes, on the grounds that a material witness, Mr. Joseph Orgill, a prisoner in the gaol who had been committed for bigamy, could not be heard in the case until he had obtained a free pardon from the Secretary of State. Owen, it was understood, had made important disclosures to Orgill while in prison. Although the counsel for Owen opposed the application, the judge consented to postpone the trial.

The judge at the second trial was Mr. Baron Gurney. There was intense public feeling locally concerning the fate of the unfortunate woman, and the avenues to the STAFFORDSHIRE ASSIZES were crowded. The case had also excited considerable interest among members of the legal profession. The three prisoners appeared at the bar in the sleeve waistcoats usually worn at that time by boatmen. They were charged with wilful murder 'by casting, pushing and throwing the said

Christina Collins into the canal, by which means she was choked, suffocated and drowned'.

[Entrance to the HARECASTLE TUNNEL at the Kidsgrove end. Brindley's original tunnel is on the right while Telford's much larger tunnel is to the left]

It seems that the journey from PRESTON BROOK to STOKE-ON-TRENT was comparatively uneventful, although Owen sat with Christina in the cabin while the boat was negotiated through the HARECASTLE TUNNEL. However, from the time that the boat reached the Potteries, things began to happen. William Brookes, a porter for the PICKFORDS COMPANY confirmed that the boat arrived at STOKE-ON-TRENT at noon on the 16th June, and that it remained there for four hours. There was a woman passenger on board, and she complained before the boat set off about the conduct of the men. He heard her say to Thomas, 'Leave me alone, I'll not have anything to do with you!'. Thomas then used some disgraceful language. The men were obviously beginning to become the worse for drink, and Brookes gave it as his opinion that they were 'making free with the spirit which was the cargo'. Many boat captains were known by boat crews for their expertise in stealing spirits so adroitly from the carboys on board that no-one could detect the interference.

Christina, in an effort to avoid the remainder of the boat journey, enquired the times of the coaches to London from STOKE-ON-TRENT, but they were not convenient. Brookes's wife travelled as a passenger on the boat from STOKE-ON-TRENT for about three-and-a-half miles, and she stated that there was a female passenger aboard who looked pale and poorly. She added that the passenger was completely sober, but was very concerned about her own safety.

Hugh Cordwell, Check Clerk to the TRENT & MERSEY CANAL at STONE, said the boat arrived there at 8.00 p.m. on the Sunday evening. Mrs. Collins complained to him that the men were now so drunk she thought they were going to 'meddle with her'. Cordwell told her to report the men at the journey's end. He noticed that Owen in particular appeared to be very drunk.

[ASTON LOCK near STONE where Christina rejoined the narrow boat after sharpening her penknife]

John Tansley, Assistant Clerk to the TRENT & MERSEY CANAL at ASTON LOCK, about a mile-and-a-half from STONE, said that the boat arrived there at 8.30.p.m. on the Sunday evening. Christina had arrived there on foot a little earlier, as she had been so frightened of the drunken boatmen that she had decided to walk along the tow-path, hoping to rejoin the boat later when the men might be sober. While she waited for the boat to come up, she sharpened a penknife on the lock keeper's cottage steps (one of the boatmen was later found to have a cut on his face, and this could have been made with the knife). As the boat drew up alongside, one of the men (Tansley did not know which) 'cursed her eyes and wished she was in hell flames, for he hated the sight of her'. As she boarded the boat at ASTON LOCK, the Captain offered Christina something to drink, but it is doubtful whether she drank it, because Samuel Barratt, the RUGELEY surgeon, who later conducted the post-mortem examination at the TALBOT INN in the town, found no evidence of alcohol in her body.

[SANDON LOCK]

Thomas Blore said he was captain of a PICKFORDS COMPANY boat which passed Owen's boat near SANDON LOCK at about 9.00 p.m. on the Sunday evening. As the boats drew alongside, Owen referred to the woman passenger in terms that were completely disgusting. He vowed, in the coarsest terms, what he would do with her that night, 'or else he would *Burke* her'. (Burke was a criminal who had been executed ten years earlier for smothering his victims and then selling their bodies for dissecting). He added that Owen was very drunk, and Thomas rather so.

At this point the terrified Christina took another walk along the tow-path to escape from the drunken men, but it is certain that she was on board again by the time the boat left SANDON LOCK at 9.50 p.m. A few minutes later she was out walking again, because Robert Walker, a boat captain, said he passed her on the tow-path just after 10.00 p.m. As he approached SANDON LOCK he met Owen's boat, and one of the men asked if he had seen a woman on the tow-path, adding in the crudest language what he would do with her when he had her in his clutches.

[Lonely HOO MILL LOCK where Christina was last seen alive]

James Mills, the keeper of the HOO MILL LOCK, said that he and his wife, Anne, were awakened by a scream of terror coming from the direction of the lock at midnight. At first they thought it was the cry of a child. They looked through the bedroom window, and saw three men by the boat in the lock and a woman on the cabin. Her legs hung down at the side of the cabin. She said in a terrified voice, 'I'll not go down. Don't attempt me!'. Anne Mills enquired who the woman was and one of the men replied 'A passenger'. He added that she had her husband with her.

No one other than the boatmen seems to have seen Christina again until her body was found at 5.00 a.m. on the Monday morning at BRINDLEY BANK, near the aqueduct in RUGELEY. Thomas Grant, a boatman, said that as he was passing by he saw something in the water.

[BRINDLEY BANK as seen from the aqueduct]

He could see a gown. It was on the side of the canal opposite the towing-path. He found it to be a body of a female, without bonnet or shoes. Her body was pointing towards PRESTON BROOK. She was lying on her face which was quite black.

[The TALBOT INN, RUGELEY]

19

He stopped his boat and with his boat-hook pulled the body over to the tow-path and lifted it out of the water with the help of John Johnson, a local wharfinger who happened to be crossing the aqueduct at the time. The body was warm. Johnson took it to the TALBOT INN, RUGELEY, (not to be confused with the Talbot Arms Inn, later the Shrewsbury Arms).

At the point where the unfortunate Christina met her death, Thomas and Owen left the boat and stood together on the bank. William Hatton passed by in his boat at the time (about 1.30 a.m. Monday) and Thomas and Owen, with great presence of mind, asked Hatton if he had seen a woman. He said 'No', but they asked the question again in rather an agitated way.

[WOOD END LOCK where the boatmen reported the drowning of Christina to the lock keeper]

John Bladon, wharfinger, in the employment of the TRENT & MERSEY CANAL, at RUGELEY, said that as the boat passed him Owen did not report the loss of a passenger, which he certainly ought to have done under the company regulations. The boatmen decided to say that their passenger had been out of her mind: that she had committed suicide; and that they had had to save her from drowning once before on the journey from Liverpool. When the boat arrived at WOOD END

[FRADLEY JUNCTION where the boatmen reported to the
PICKFORDS COMPANY clerk]

[COLWICH LOCK where Christina was supposed to have drowned
according to the boatmen. Just visible behind the cottage is the main
railway line to London]

LOCK, near King's Bromley, at about 5.30 a.m. on the Monday, Owen called at the house of John Lee, the lock keeper, and told him and his wife, Ann, that a passenger of theirs had been drowned, but that she was deranged. Owen was trembling badly, and appeared very confused. He was obviously drunk.

At FRADLEY JUNCTION, a little further on, Owen told Charles Robotham, the PICKFORDS COMPANY clerk there, 'A very bad job has happened. A passenger has drowned herself. She was 'off her head'. We last saw her at COLWICH LOCK'. Owen was unwilling to go back towards COLWICH LOCK with Robotham and this made the clerk suspicious. He therefore went as quickly as he could to FAZELEY, the next stop, where William Kirk, the PICKFORDS COMPANY agent, sent for the police. When the boat arrived, two hours behind schedule, Thomas was still very drunk. William Harrison, the constable, took the crew into custody and testified that the men were all 'tipsy' and abusive as he handcuffed them. One of them muttered, 'Damn and blast the woman'.

THE VERDICT

The local constabulary had not been established at the date of the murder; it was still a few years away. Constables were appointed on an *ad hoc* basis, as felt by the local magistrates to be necessary.

Hannah Phillips of RUGELEY testified that at the TALBOT INN she was employed to take off Christina's clothes. The left sleeve was ripped out of its gathers and the cuff on one hand was also ripped. Small chintz muslin handkerchiefs on each shoulder were also ripped. Grant and Johnson were certain that they made no tears in the clothing as they lifted the body from the canal.

Elizabeth Matthews said she helped Hannah Phillips to take off Christina's clothes. She particularly noticed the state of the calico drawers, which were torn right across the front. They were produced in court.

Samuel Barratt, the RUGELEY surgeon, who examined the body at the inquest, said there were two bruises below the elbow, near the wrist of the right arm. In his opinion death was occasioned by suffocation and drowning.

Musson, the young boy, gave his version of the story. He was certain that Ellis was asleep at the time of the murder, for he had heard him snoring. We shall never know whether Ellis had forced him to say this, under threat of punishment.

Joseph Orgill, the man for whose evidence the re-trial had been ordered, related what Owen had told him while they were both together in the prison cell. In essence it was an attempt by Owen to blame the other two men for all that had happened, but the story made no impression on the jury.

The knife Christina sharpened was later found in one of her trunks, the cord of which had been untied. It was assumed that the men had opened her belongings after the murder, and had placed the knife in the trunk. It is conceivable that the men intended to steal her belongings, for a charge of theft was included in the indictment at the first trial.

But of all the evidence given in court that of Robert Collins evoked the greatest feelings. He was weeping aloud as he entered the witness box, and seemed as though he could hardly bear the sight of the prisoners. He had obviously been deeply in love with Christina, and explained how he identified the body by a mark on her ear.

At the conclusion of the hearing and the summing up by the judge, the jury, under their chairman, Mr. Edward Walley of Hanley, retired to consider their verdict. They were unanimous in pronouncing the three boatmen guilty of murder.

The black coif, emblematical of death, was placed on the judge's head. The prisoners were asked if they had anything to say. Then the judge passed sentence as follows:

'James Owen, George Thomas and William Ellis, after a long and patient hearing of the circumstances of this case, and after due deliberation on the part of the jury, you have been found guilty of the foul crime of murder, murder of an unoffending and helpless woman who was under your protection and who, there is reason to believe, was the object of your lust; and then, to prevent detection for that crime, was the object of your cruelty. Look not for pardon in this world. Apply to the God of Mercy for that pardon which He alone can extend to penitent sinners, and prepare yourselves for the ignominious death which awaits you. This case is one of the most shocking that has ever come under my knowledge, and it remains for me to pass upon you the awful sentence of the Law, that you be taken from whence you came, and from thence to the place of execution, and that you and each of you, be hanged by the neck until you are dead, and that your bodies afterwards be buried within the precincts of the prison. And may God have mercy on your souls'.

After the trial was over, the men persisted in maintaining their innocence. Owen was visited in prison by his wife, who was so agitated 'as to be thrown into a fit'.

It seems fairly certain, from the statements of Owen and Thomas, that Ellis had been much less involved in the happenings on the canal journey than the other two men had been. Some members of the legal profession now thought there was a case for the last-minute reconsideration of the sentence imposed upon Ellis, so a letter setting forth their view was taken to London by a barrister, and a special interview with the Secretary of State was obtained. As a result of these representations, Ellis was reprieved. The news was broken to him just as the three men were receiving for the last time the Sacrament from the prison chaplain. Ellis immediately burst into tears, and taking each of his former associates by the hand, kissed them affectionately, repeating, 'God bless you, dear boys'.

The commuted sentence of Ellis was that he should be transported to Australia for the rest of his life. He was returned initially to STAFFORD

COUNTY GAOL, where he became a changed character. His transformation was such that both the prison governor and the chaplain were moved to write separate letters to the visiting magistrates to the prison, pointing out Ellis's current conduct, and enquiring whether the transportation sentence might come under review. The governor's letter read as follows:

TO THE VISITING MAGISTRATES OF THE COUNTY
PRISON AT STAFFORD

My Lords and Gentlemen,

Understanding it is your pleasure to recommend the Court of Quarter Sessions to apply for Her Majesty's Pardon for William Ellis, who was convicted of murder at the Spring Assizes, 1840 (with two other persons since executed) and who now remains in this Prison under sentence of transportation for the remainder of his life, I beg most respectfully to report his conduct during the very long time he has been in my custody. It is now nearly two years and a half since he was committed for trial, at which period he was an ignorant man and not capable of reading and writing, but since his conviction he has applied himself so strenuously of his own free will and desire to improve himself that for some time past he has been able to read well, and write tolerably so, and his general conduct during the whole of his imprisonment has been most exemplary. I must therefore take leave to recommend him to your favourable consideration, as a reformed man and a deserving object of the Royal Clemency.

I have the honour to be, my Lords and Gentlemen, your most obedient and humble servant,

Thos. Bruton,
Governor.

16th October,1841.

The result of this intervention was that Ellis's transportation sentence was reduced from life to fourteen years, but it seems certain that he went to Australia.

[Gateway to STAFFORD COUNTY GAOL in the 19th century (top) and as seen in 2010 (bottom)]

Owen and Thomas were hanged in public at STAFFORD COUNTY GAOL on 11th April 1840. According to the newspaper reports, nearly ten thousand people were present to witness the macabre spectacle. They sat on walls, climbed trees, and even perched themselves on the roofs of nearby houses in order to obtain a good view. At the appointed time, 'the chaplain appeared first, reading the funeral service of the Church of England; followed by the two culprits, the executioner, and the governor and officers of the prison. The men walked with a firm step, and ascended the steps of the drop without assistance. The executioner, immediately placed the ropes around their necks, shook hands with them and as the chaplain pronounced the words, 'In the midst of life we are in death'. The fatal bolt was drawn, and the wretched men ceased to live. Their bodies were much convulsed'.

[William Calcraft the hangman]

The hangman was William Calcraft, who toured the provinces as need arose doing provincial hangings for £10 a time. Calcraft had, earlier in his working life, been a shoemaker, but later worked at Newgate, flogging young offenders for ten shillings (50p) a week. In 1829 he was appointed executioner, to replace John Foxton, who had died of alcohol poisoning. Calcraft's pay included a standard rate of one guinea (105p) per week, plus ten shillings (50p) for each execution in London, and two-shillings-and-sixpence (twelve-and-a-half pence) for each flogging, with an allowance for birch rods.

[George Smith, who replaced Thomas Cheshire as hangman's assistant, dressed for a hanging]

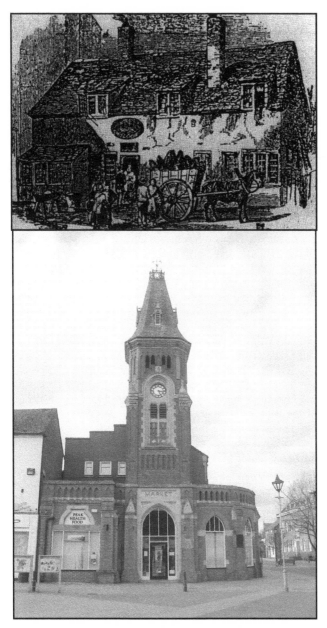

[The SHOULDER OF MUTTON INN (top) was located where the
clock tower in RUGELEY now stands (bottom)]

Calcraft's assistant was Thomas Cheshire, and when Calcraft came to STAFFORD to hang the boatmen he asked Cheshire to join him there. Cheshire had many relatives in RUGELEY, and, according to the story, he decided to mix business with pleasure by calling on his relatives on his way to STAFFORD. But none of them wished to meet a man who was assistant to the common hangman, so he decided to visit the SHOULDER OF MUTTON INN – which stood where the town clock now stands and which was demolished in 1878 when the clock tower was built – and here he became so drunk that he forgot all about his STAFFORD appointment.

Calcraft didn't like Cheshire at the best of times, but his feelings were not improved when his assistant failed to arrive. Good hangmen's assistants were not easy to obtain, so Calcraft appealed for help to the STAFFORD COUNTY GAOL governor, Thomas Bruton. After due consideration, the governor felt that the only possibility would be to ask one of his prisoners, George Smith – who was in prison for debt – if he would like to fill the gap, providing Calcraft settled his debt. Smith agreed quickly, and thus Calcraft obtained a new assistant who was to take readily to his work. Smith's task during an execution was to go below the platform and be ready, should Calcraft signal, to jump up and hang on to the legs of the victims when the *drop* didn't kill them quickly enough.

Eventually, Smith became a hangman in his own right, and he considered his crowning achievement to be the execution of Dr. William Palmer, 'RUGELEY poisoner', in 1856.

After hanging for the usual hour, the boatmen's bodies were cut down, and buried within the gaol. Locally produced broadsheets, giving details of the trial and execution, were soon on sale in the streets. They even gave details of the sermons that were preached to the men on the Sunday before their execution. One such sermon, based on the text, 'flee from the wrath to come', concluded:

'You, my fellow men, who are now treading on the awful verge of Eternity, whose ears will never more listen to the pleadings of mercy, I would charge with the most solemn emphasis to 'flee from the wrath to come'. You cannot escape the sentence of the violated laws, but oh! There is another Judge who will execute justice, but whose ears are never closed to the cries of the penitent. Entreat pardon from Him, and He is ready to blot out your transgressions. There is no time for delay, but 'flee from the wrath to come' (Matthew 3.7)'.

At the foot of the broad sheet was a representation of Christina being molested by the boatmen at HOO MILL LOCK. The lock keeper's

[Christina being molested by the boatmen]

wife had been awakened by her screams, and she is pictured looking
through the bedroom window. On either side of the illustration, the story
is told in verse, as follows:

> Good Christian people, pray attend
> Whilst I relate to you
> Concerning of a murder foul,
> It is, alas, too true.
>
> A helpless female, much beloved
> Was travelling to her home,
> Three boatmen seized her as she sat
> The water was her home.
>
> A letter she had just received
> From her beloved friend,
> It was her husband, you shall hear
> That did for her then send.
>
> Upon the water she did go,
> It was the nearest way,
> But sad to tell she never more
> Did see the light of day.
>
> James Owen then did her affright,
> The wretched woman cried,
> Dobell he said "'Tis all in vain,
> All help it is denied".

31

Ellis he then assisted them,
They bruised her body sore,
Their hearts did never once relent
Till life it was no more.

THE LIVES TRIAL & EXECUTION,
OF PICKFORD'S TWO BOATMEN,

Who Suffered Apirl the 11th, 1840 at Stafford, for the Wilful Murder of Christina Collins, near Rugeley, on the 17th, of June 1839. Together with OWEN'S CONFESSION,

The Execution of Owen, and Thomas, in Front of the Goal.

THE EXECUTION.

WRIGHT. Printer, Birmingham

[The locally produced broadsheet as sold in the streets of STAFFORD]

32

'Twas on the 17th day of June
This murder it was done.
They did complete the awful deed
Before the rising sun.

Loud were her shrieks, but all was vain,
She all her strength did try,
To save her life she struggled long,
But now she was to die.

Her voice grew faint, life's ebbing stream
Did flow upon the boat,
The glassy eye convinced them all
That they the deed had wrought.

They threw the body overboard
To hide the crime they'd done,
But Providence did so ordain
The body should be found.

In Staffordshire these monsters were,
In Rugeley, you shall hear,
They now in prison lie condemned,
Their sentence is past here.

Christina Collins lost her life
By their most ruthless hand,
May God prepare them all in time
To meet at His right hand.

CHRISTINA'S LEGACY

The horror felt by the local population at the murder of the unfortunate Christina did not end with the hanging of the men. Many people felt that something should be done to try to improve the morals of the boatmen on all the canals. Many were sorry that the boatmen had to work on Sundays, and that they therefore had no opportunity to go to church. A letter to the local press from the Vicar of Haughton was typical of many. He wondered how far the employers of the boatmen were to blame for not allowing these men time off from their duties to go to church on Sundays.

Every member of the coroner's jury, after the original coroner's inquest, at the TALBOT INN, RUGELEY, in June 1839, felt strongly, too, about the morals of the boatmen. They were moved to express their feelings in writing, and addressed a letter to the coroner, as follows:

Mr. Coroner,

Now that this long and painful investigation is closed, we, the undersigned, who have attended your inquest on the body of Christina Collins, beg to state that we are not satisfied to separate without first strongly expressing our decided conviction of the great impropriety of the carrying business both by land and water being carried upon the Sunday in the same manner as the other days.

The evidence that has been brought before us has brought under our observation much of what appears to be the usual conversation and demeanour of boatmen, and we concede that the narration will not only excite the abhorrence of all respectable persons, but that it is highly disgraceful to the community at large so long as the community has not done its utmost to stay the evil. By the violation of the Sabbath, not only boatmen but also great numbers of other persons who are engaged in the conveyance of goods and also employed as clerks and porters, are entirely prevented from paying attention to religious duties on the day expressly set apart for that purpose, and their children are deprived of those instructions which are afforded to other children of their rank in life.

We further beg to state that we cannot but attribute the great demoralisation which is proved to exist among boatmen principally to these causes, and we think it is more than probable that had the unfortunate men who have been the subject of this investigation been compelled to keep the Sabbath

---

day, insofar as human laws can be available to this end, the late deplorable event might not have occurred.

With this consideration, Sir, we feel that we should be failing in our duty were we not to remonstrate as strongly as we can against the continuance of the present system, and we beg of you, Sir, to make known these our sentiments to the proper quarter.

William Turner (Foreman)	Thomas Masters
John Thomas Walkers	Henry Collet
John Jackness	James Moxon
Thomas Dicken	Thomas Phillips
Henry Walter Holland	John Cheshire
Robert Bullock	John Britain.

This local concern for the boatmen and their working conditions led to the well-known nineteenth century Vicar of Kidsgrove, North Staffordshire, the Reverend Tobias Wade, being called to give evidence at the 1841 Select Committee on Sunday Trading. Mr. Wade lived in very close proximity to the HARECASTLE TUNNEL, on the TRENT & MERSEY CANAL, on the Staffordshire – Cheshire border, and he had ample opportunity to speak to the boatmen and their families, with whom he had much sympathy. From his observations, the boatmen were nearly all illiterate and of low intelligence. They would love the opportunity to have a twenty-four hour break on Sundays, so that they could spend time with their families and attend church. Some of the more progressive employers had in fact conceded this break for their workpeople, but others had not, and it caused friction between employers and their crews.

Some of the boatmen's young children, and also teenage sons and daughters, were prepared to attend a special school started by Mr. Wade, but they would not attend the village school at Kidsgrove, for fear of being ridiculed for their ignorance by the village children.

Although the boatmen were ignorant of the Bible, they listened very attentively to the sermons given by Mr. Wade and his chaplain, and many of them became reformed, sober characters. A large number of the boatmen had run away from their homes when they were young, perhaps because they had committed improper acts, and they came to the canal in the knowledge that they could obtain employment without any questions being asked. It was quite common for these men to change their names when they obtained canal employment, so as to avoid detection.

The churches and chapels in general became active in many areas of the canal system, in trying to end the depraved life-style of the boatmen, and a nineteenth century Bishop of Lichfield, Bishop Selwyn, started a mobile canal mission to boatmen.

[The current 'Bloody Steps' leading down to BRINDLEY BANK]

At the point where the body of Christina Collins was taken from the canal, there was a flight of sandstone steps (since replaced by a parallel flight of concrete steps), and a local tradition had it that blood from the

37

body stained the steps indelibly. Ever since, the flight of steps – including the modern replacement flight – has been known as the 'Bloody Steps' by generations of Rugeleians. There is, of course, no truth in the story. The 'blood marks' were simply markings on the sandstone.

The area around the steps and the canal at this point are still held in some awe by many local people. Some have seen strange things and heard strange voices in the area. One lady told the author that as she was climbing the 'Bloody Steps' one evening she heard a voice at her shoulder. She turned sharply, but saw nothing. But perhaps the strangest story occurred about fifty years ago, when, one summer's evening just before the outbreak of World War II, Mrs. Southwell and her mother from Arch Street, RUGELEY, were walking in the vicinity of the 'Bloody Steps'. They gave the local paper, the *Rugeley Times* – now defunct – details of what happened when they saw the ghostly figure of a man walking towards them:

> "He seemed to glide over the lawn, and when he came to the railings, he passed through them", said Mrs. Southwell. "He was dressed in black and white, with his hair, long and black, tied with a ribbon at the back of the neck. His trousers were like knickerbockers, and below his knee he appeared to be in a mist. We saw his sad face, but he said nothing"'.

Later that day, the two ladies walked past SAINT AUGUSTINE'S CHURCH in RUGELEY, and something impelled them to look at the inscription on Christina's headstone. They were amazed to realise that the ghostly appearance had taken place exactly one hundred years ago to the day after the murder. The identity of the ghost was the subject of speculation but was not established.

Popular photography did not exist at the time of Christina's murder, and no photograph of her was ever taken. But, according to an article in the 1839 *STAFFORDSHIRE GAZETTE*, in Christina's trunk was found 'a half length portrait of him (Collins) in oil, tolerably executed, and a painting of the deceased (Christina)'. How fascinating it would be if these paintings ever came to light.

GAZETTEER

ASTON LOCK

The village of Aston is located in a tranquil part of Staffordshire, near STONE on the TRENT & MERSEY CANAL. A new feature of this area close to Aston Lock is the twelve-acre, one-hundred-and-eighty berth Aston Marina that offers boat repairs as well as boasting easy access for narrow boats.

BODLEIAN LIBRARY (OXFORD)

This is the main research library of the University of Oxford and also one of the oldest libraries in Europe, and in Britain is second in size only to the British Library. Under the *Legal Deposit Libraries Act 2003* it is one of six legal deposit libraries for works published in the United Kingdom and hence it is entitled to request a copy of each book published in the country. Though University members may borrow some books from dependent libraries (such as the Radcliffe Science Library), the Bodleian Library operates principally as a reference library and in general documents may not be removed from the reading rooms.

BRINDLEY BANK (RUGELEY)

Brindley Bank is known not only as the place where the body of Christina Collins was found (as noted by a British Waterways sign indicating the spot) but also for its aqueduct. The Brindley Bank aqueduct is a four-arched structure that James Brindley (after whom the area is named) built to carry the TRENT & MERSEY CANAL over the River Trent. This major feat of civil engineering by Brindley was achieved by first building half the structure on dry land, and then excavating a channel used to divert the river under the new structure. This enabled the other half to be built on dry land and when complete the river was let go so that it could flow along both its natural and man-made channels. This technique had the advantage of increasing the size of the channel to provide capacity for floodwater.

All of Brindley's aqueducts are characterised by being very broad and sturdy structures because they had to withstand the weight of water as well as the mass of clay puddle used to contain them. In the case of Brindley Bank the canal was designed to follow the natural contours of the land as much as possible and at this point the River Trent should have been crossed on the slant. Instead, the crossing was made at 90° because the technology to build skew arches, that could transmit lateral thrust to the abutments, had not yet been developed. Consequently Brindley always made river crossings at 90° and in this instance the canal also has a 90° bend in it at one end (as seen in the picture on page 19).

Although the Brindley Bank aqueduct is substantial it was not the longest that he built on the TRENT & MERSEY CANAL that being the nine-arched aqueduct, which takes the canal over the River Dove at Clay Mills, near Burton-upon-Trent, Staffordshire.

CASTLE INN (WOLVERHAMPTON)

Originally Wolverhampton Guildhall was the only venue for plays and variety shows in the area but in 1768 an assembly room was built at the Castle Inn located in what is now George Street. In 1787 it is recorded that the club/assembly room was being used as a meeting place for members of the Congregationalist Church (Independents) that later became the United Reformed Church. This arrangement lasted up until 1795. It was also a meeting place for Methodists and in 1790 in the loft over the stables Charles Wesley preached to the congregation. However, the venue was seen as being too small and the Methodists soon relocated their meetings to a larger room over the stables at the Dragon Inn. Hence it may be inferred that Ingleby did not play to huge audiences in Wolverhampton.

COLWICH LOCK

Located between Colwich and Little Haywood villages Colwich Lock on the TRENT & MERSEY CANAL is less than four miles from the RUGELEY visitor moorings to the southeast and just over a mile to Haywood Lock to the northwest. It is termed a narrow lock being built by James Brindley between 1766 and 1770 consisting of a brick chamber with stone coping and quoins with a single steel top gate and double steel bottom gates. The lock rise is six-and-a half feet. The cottage for the lock keeper is a grade II listed structure.

COVENTRY CANAL

The Coventry Canal leaves the TRENT & MERSEY CANAL at FRADLEY JUNCTION and runs for thirty-eight miles up thirteen locks to Coventry where at Hawkesbury Junction it joins the OXFORD CANAL. It is neither long nor outstandingly attractive but it was, and still is, an important link between the northern and southern canal networks over which Christina Collins would have travelled.

CROSSHALL STREET (LIVERPOOL)

Crosshall Street, not to be confused with Great Crosshall Street around half a mile away, is adjacent to Dale Street in the very heart of the city of Liverpool.

Although not much is known about Crosshall Street itself, Dale Street remained for much of its life a narrow and crowded thoroughfare and was the principal location for the large packhorse and coaching inns that provided lodgings and board for travellers and changes of horse for the coaches. These included the Saracen's Head, the Golden Lion, the Golden Fleece and the Woolpack all of which disappeared during the commercial expansion of the area in the nineteenth century. Indeed it became the major route out of Liverpool for all traffic going to Warrington and southward towards London, which rather begs the question as to why Christina Collins did not simply take the coach albeit more expensive. The picture of No. 3 Crosshall Street on page 12 shows a fine example of the type of commercial building typical of the Victorian era and it may be assumed therefore that at the time Christina Collins worked here that it was almost new.

EDGWARE ROAD (LONDON)

Edgware Road is a major street that connects Marble Arch in the City of Westminster to, as its name suggests, Edgware in the London Borough of Barnet. Originally it was a Roman road (Watling Street) through the Great Middlesex Forest but today is part of the A5 trunk road and noted at the southern end for its distinct Middle Eastern cuisine and many late-night bars and *shisha* cafes being often referred to locally as Little Cairo, Little Beirut and Little Cyprus.

In 1711 the road was improved by the Edgware-Kilburn turnpike trust and as a consequence a number of the local inns became stops for coaches. Hence Robert Collins would have been ideally placed to find work as an ostler in the area, particularly since the location of his lodgings at No. 10 would have been close to Marble Arch.

At that time the road would have been to the 1811 Thomas Telford design with the main occupants being Huguenot migrants who gave way late in the nineteenth century to Arab migrants due to the increased trade with the Ottoman Empire.

By the 1950s the area expanded with an influx of Egyptians and has hence always been a place of ethnic culture.

FAZELEY

Fazeley is a small town and civil parish in the District of Lichfield, Staffordshire, being located on the outskirts of Tamworth. It sits astride the junction of the COVENTRY CANAL with the Birmingham & Fazeley Canal, and indeed at Fazeley Junction there are a couple of period multi-storey mills still standing. Adjacent to Fazeley, rather appropriately given that it was from here that William Kirk sent for the police, is Drayton Manor, now a theme park and zoo, that was formerly the home of Robert Peel, Prime Minister and the person responsible for establishing the Metropolitan Police Force by an Act of Parliament in 1829.

FRADLEY JUNCTION

The canalside settlement at Fradley Junction, five miles east of Lichfield, was established after the COVENTRY CANAL was linked to the TRENT & MERSEY CANAL in 1790 and hence was a major junction on the Victorian canal network. Both the TRENT & MERSEY CANAL and the COVENTRY CANAL companies built houses and cottages for their workers, while two warehouses, complete with hoists, were erected at Junction Row alongside the Swan public house. Today the public house, two shops and two cafes are often teeming with gongoozlers and other visitors. Close to the junction is Fradley Nature Reserve which is also well worth a visit.

HARECASTLE TUNNEL

Situated on the TRENT & MERSEY CANAL at Kidsgrove in Staffordshire the Harecastle Tunnel is actually made up of two separate, parallel, tunnels called the Brindley (two-thousand-eight-hundred-and-eighty yards) and the Telford (two-thousand-nine-hundred-and-twenty-six yards) after the engineers that constructed them.

Today only the later Telford tunnel is navigable which is a pity since both tunnels are only wide enough to carry traffic in one direction at a time and boats are therefore sent through in groups, alternating northbound and southbound with ventilation being handled by three large fans at the southern portal. In fact there are three tunnels since above the two canal tunnels is the railway tunnel that also traverses Harecastle Hill.

At the time (1770-1777) that the Brindley tunnel was constructed it was twice as long as any other tunnel in the world although James Brindley died before it was completed. To build the canal, the line of the tunnel was ranged over the hill and then fifteen vertical shafts were sunk into the ground. It was from these that heads were driven on the canal line. A major problem was the change in the rock type that ranged from soft earth to millstone grit. The construction site was subject to regular flooding, despite the presence of steam-operated pumps, and stoves were installed at the bottom of each upcast pipe to overcome the problem of ventilation. The tunnel was twelve feet tall and just nine feet wide with no tow-path so boatmen had to 'leg' their way through the tunnel, a task that could take upwards of three hours, while the boat horses were led over Harecastle Hill via Boathorse Road. Even at the time it was too small for the amount of traffic, while in 1914 there was a partial collapse with the resultant closure for good and the gating up of the entrances.

In recent times, water entering the canal from the Brindley tunnel has been blamed for much of the prominent iron ore in the canal (as evident from the rusty colour of the water), and there are proposals to install filtering (possibly using reed beds) at the northern portal.

The larger Telford tunnel, which originally had a towpath that sank below the water line as the tunnel settled, was opened in 1827, at a cost of £113,000, after just three years work and illustrates the engineering advances that had been made since Brindley's time. Between 1914 and 1954 horse power gave way to an electric tug that was used to pull boats through the tunnel at a cost of 6d per boat, whereas it cost 1/6d to 'leg' it through the Brindley tunnel (due to the time consideration). In 1954 the three large fans were constructed at the southern portal. While all the boats are within the tunnel an airtight door is shut and all the air is pulled through the tunnel by the fan. This allows diesel boats to use the tunnel without suffocating the boaters. Today the journey takes about thirty to forty minutes, and there are around six thousand such journeys (mainly by pleasure craft) per year.

However, in the late twentieth century, the Telford tunnel also began to suffer subsidence, and was closed between 1973 and 1977. The towpath, long disused and under water, was removed, allowing boats to take advantage of the greater air draft in the centre of the tunnel. Interestingly a series of smaller canal tunnels are joined to the Telford tunnel. These tunnels connected to the coal mines at Golden Hill and allowed both the drainage of the mines and the export of coal directly from the mines to the canal tunnel without the necessity of first hauling it to the surface. Small boats of ten tons capacity were used in this endeavour.

It is not clear which of the tunnels Christina Collins would have passed through since both were in operation at the time, although it is recorded that she sat in the cabin with Owen, the captain, who might well have told her the legend of a young woman who was said to have been decapitated in the Telford tunnel with her body thrown into Gilbert's Hole, a coal landing stage within the tunnel. It seems that a man had hacked the woman's head from her shoulders with a piece of slate, and like all good stories it was said that the ghost of the woman, known as the 'Kidsgrove Boggart', now haunts Harecastle Tunnel, either in the form of a headless woman, or a white horse, and her appearance fore-warns of disaster in the local mines. Some boatmen even took long detours to avoid the tunnel and today the tunnel keepers relate tales of occasional mismatches in the number of boats going in and coming out of the tunnel. However, there is no record of any such murder, and it is not even known when the story came into existence and may even have been inspired by the murder of Christina Collins herself.

HOO MILL LOCK

This is lock No. 23 on the TRENT & MERSEY CANAL being close to Great Haywood Junction to the south and some nine miles from STONE to the northwest. The lock rise is nearly eight feet. The lock cottage, from where Christina Collins was last seen alive, was recently valued at £366,000 having been last on the market in 1996 when it sold for £136,000.

LYCEUM THEATRE (LONDON)

There has been a Lyceum Theatre in Wellington Street, just off the Strand, since 1765, with the present building being opened on 14th July 1834 to a design by Samuel Beazley. Indeed it is unique in having a balcony overhanging the circle. Although the façade and grand portico are the same today the rest is substantially different and dates from the 1904 design of Bertie Crewe.

Ingleby though would have performed at the old Lyceum Theatre (adjacent to the current building) that between 1794 and 1809 amongst other uses became a circus, having been brought by Philip Astley when his amphitheatre was burned down at Westminster. In 1802 it became the first venue for an exhibition of waxworks by one Madame Tussaud.

NEW RADFORD (NOTTINGHAMSHIRE)

Although it is stated that Christina Collins was born in New Radford this strictly speaking is not true for New Radford did not exist in 1801. Indeed prior 1796 when one Benjamin Darker, needle-maker, built four houses the entire parish from Old Badford church to the top of Derby Road was just fields and gardens. He subsequently built nine more dwellings having paid two shillings per yard for the land. All the buildings were insured with the Phoenix Fire Office but the district mentioned in the policy was New Weston, not New Radford. It was a very basic place to live with there being no sewers, and many years passed before there was much advance with regard to water supply.

However, in 1824 Joshua Beardmore, a tallow-chandler, sunk a well in Holden Street, sixty yards deep, and with a steam engine pumped water into a tank, and sent a man round with a cart selling the water at a halfpenny a bucket. He afterwards established a water works at Sion Hill and installed a system of pipes under the streets. He subsequently sold the whole enterprise to Messrs. Walker, and they continued the supply, only ceasing on payment of £5,000 compensation for the goodwill of supplying water to the people of what was now called New Radford and the Park. Later the area became known for its great factories for the manufacture of lace, cotton doubling, hosiery, embroideries, bobbins and carriages, and other industries and hence it can be understood just how the Brown family became involved with that industry.

NOTTINGHAM JOURNAL

The *Nottingham Journal* was established in 1710 as a weekly publication with Whig sympathies although the phrase 'Independent – Liberal' was tacked onto the title indicating that Conservatives with Liberal views were also targeted as readers.

OXFORD CANAL

The Oxford Canal, initially designed by James Brindley, succeeded by Samuel Simcock and Robert Whitworth after Brindley's untimely death in 1772 at the age of fifty-six was one of the first to be built in the country. It was opened in sections between 1774 and 1790 with the purpose of bringing coal from the Coventry coalfields to Oxford and the River Thames, and was part of Brindley's grand plan for a waterway connecting the Thames, Mersey, Trent and Severn rivers.

The Oxford Canal provided a direct link with London via the River Thames, and for several years was hugely profitable. The arrival of the Grand Junction Canal, linking Braunston (where key scenes in the film version of Colin Dexter's book *The Wench is Dead* were filmed) to London and later becoming the backbone of the Grand Union Canal, finally broke its stranglehold and effectively bypassed the southern half of the Oxford Canal.

Nonetheless, it brought more traffic to the northern section, which soon required upgrading. The Oxford Canal was originally built to the contour method favoured by Brindley, which not only meant that the level remained fairly constant, but that the canal could call at many villages and wharves along the route. The drawback to this approach was the lengthy transit times.

In the 1830s Marc Brunel and William Cubitt made the most of developments in engineering to straighten Brindley's original line, resulting in several 'loops', where the new line bisected the old. Other improvements included the duplication of locks at Hillmorton, and widening of the stretch between Napton and Braunston, where the canal shares its route with the Grand Union Canal. Today the southern section between Napton and Oxford remains remarkably unspoilt and offers an evocative insight into canal life as it would have been two centuries ago.

PICKFORDS COMPANY

As a moving business the family firm of Pickfords is believed to have been founded in the seventeenth century, making it one of the oldest functioning companies in the country. The earliest record is of a William Pickford, a carrier who worked south of Manchester in 1630, while in 1646 a north-country yeoman by the name of Thomas Pickford had his lands confiscated by Parliament for gun-running and supporting the Cavaliers during the English Civil War. Meanwhile the Pickford family of Adlington, south of Manchester, and later of nearby Poynton, also entered the wagon trade in the seventeenth century.

Certainly by 1695 members of one branch of the Pickford family were engaged in supplying quarry stone by packhorse for the construction of turnpike roads; instead of the packhorses returning with empty loads, they carried goods for third parties, and hence for profit.

In 1756 the company relocated to London and in 1776 it invented the fly wagon that could travel from London to Manchester in the then fast speed of four-and-a-half days. A year later it bought the carrier business of William Bass, a Staffordshire haulier who carried ale for a local brewer. With the funds Bass went on to form the brewery that still bears his name today.

In the 1779 Pickfords (note use of the plural indicating more than one Pickford family or member) entered the canal industry (from which it withdrew in 1850). Also at this time the company operated wagons on other companies' railways, but this was contentious, and eventually this service ceased. Despite the rapid expansions all was not well with the company and in 1816 the company was close to bankruptcy after many years of decline. The family sold out to a number of businessmen led by Joseph Baxendale, whose family become instrumental in running the company for over a century, so in fact at the time when Christina Collins was on a Pickfords boat it was no longer owned by the family.

In the twentieth century the company switched to road haulage, and during this time it formed a rivalry with fellow hauliers Carter Paterson, with whom (amongst others) they merged in 1912, although both kept their separate names. In 1920 the company was sold again, to Hays

Wharf Limited, on the back of a burgeoning post-World War I home removals business. In turn Hays Wharf was taken over by the four main British railway companies in 1934 and was subsequently nationalised in 1947 as part of British Road Services and what would become the National Freight Corporation (NFC) in the 1969.

As part of the NFC Pickfords was involved in a wide range of haulage activities including heavy haulage (moving oversize loads) from the 1950s to the 1980s. The company absorbed several other well-known haulage companies during this period but then withdrew from the sector. Some former Pickfords vehicles from this era have been preserved and can today be seen at events, demonstrating moving outsize loads along with the earlier steam tractors.

The company was sold again in 1982, 1996, 2002 and 2008 while in 2009 what was now Allied Pickfords, the international arm of the company, reverted to the original name of just Pickfords. The domestic part of the operation is now part of Moving Services Group UK, and as a whole is the largest moving group in the country, with fifty-six branches serving every postcode in the United Kingdom and Ireland. The company provides a complete portfolio of services to consumers and businesses including domestic removals, moving overseas, moving to Europe, business moving, transition and project management, employee moving services, small moves and packing materials.

PRESTON BROOK

Preston Brook is a civil parish in the borough of Halton, Cheshire and located to the southeast of Runcorn adjacent to the M56 motorway. It contains the villages of Preston Brook and Preston on the Hill. Today approximately three thousand people are employed in the area.

The Bridgewater Canal runs from Manchester through Preston Brook where it divides into two branches. One branch leads to Runcorn where it used to join the Manchester Ship Canal, and before that the River Mersey, while the other branch joins the TRENT & MERSEY CANAL at the Preston Brook tunnel.

The building of the canal was authorised in 1766, and its construction came under the control of the Duke of Bridgewater. Either by accident or design he built the Preston Brook tunnel too narrow to take the wide Mersey Flat boats. The connection to the TRENT & MERSEY CANAL was made just ten metres inside the northern end of the tunnel in 1772. This stretch of the canal was opened in 1776 and the Duke was able to build a number of trans-shipment warehouses to move goods to and from smaller boats which enabled him to charge unloading, loading and warehouse fees as well as transit charges giving him large profits. The canal and its warehouses were a very busy commercial area for the next hundred years, and hence this is why Christina Collins needed to transfer boats here in order to continue her journey from Liverpool to London.

At first trade was encouraged by the arrival of the railways in 1837, and Preston Brook's location on the Warrington to Chester road. However, it was also the railways that sounded the death knell of the commercial canals. One or two of the warehouses can still be seen today but most have long since been demolished.

From 1781 horse-drawn boats carried passengers between Runcorn and Manchester, stopping at Preston Brook to meet the Chester coach. The journey took seven hours and you could either travel by 'best cabin' with plush seats and tea and cakes elegantly served for three shillings, or in the 'after cabin' with wooden benches for two shillings. A faster two-horse boat was introduced in 1843 cutting the journey time in half. The boats ran until 1872 when the train finally won over all the passenger traffic. From its opening until 1865 boats were horse drawn and 'legged' through the Preston Brook tunnel. After that steam tugs were employed to pull the boats through but this resulted in a number of boatmen being overcome by fumes so traffic was stopped until ventilation shafts were built.

RUGELEY

Rugeley is a historic market town, with a population of over twenty thousand people, in the county of Staffordshire at the northern edge of Cannock Chase, and is located roughly midway between the towns of STAFFORD, Cannock, Lichfield, and Uttoxeter.

The town was a centre of coal mining until 1991, when the Lea Hall colliery was demolished, although the skyline is still dominated by Rugeley B coal-fired power station. The town was mentioned as Rudgeley in the Domesday Book being a corruption of 'ridge lee' (the hill over the field), and before coal the town thrived on iron workings and glass production during the medieval period.

Whereas most towns can boast famous inhabitants Rugeley is perhaps unfortunate in being associated with three infamous events, one of which of course was the murder of Christina Collins. It was in 1855 some years after the Christina Collins affair, that the town again found notoriety when a local doctor, William Palmer, was accused of murdering an acquaintance, John Parsons Cook (who is buried in a still visible grave at the local SAINT AUGUSTINE'S CHURCH, the same churchyard as where Christina Collins is also interred). It was claimed that Cook had been poisoned, and in the months that followed, Palmer was implicated in the deaths of several other persons, including his own wife and brother, and possibly even some of his own children. He was put on trial for the murder of Cook in 1856, and an Act of Parliament was passed to allow the trial to be held at the Old Bailey in London, as it was felt that a fair jury could not be found in Staffordshire. Palmer was found guilty of murder, and hanged publicly outside STAFFORD COUNTY GAOL on 14th June 1856. Local legend has it that, on being instructed to step on to the gallows trap-door he asked the now famous question, "Is it safe?" Furthermore, following the uproar surrounding the discovery of Palmer's activities, the town put in a special request to the Prime Minister requesting that they be permitted to change the name of the town to disassociate themselves from the murders. Unfortunately, the Prime Minister at the time was Lord Palmerston, who agreed to the request only on the condition that the town be named after himself. For obvious reasons the locals declined this offer. The story of Palmer was told in the film *The Life and Crimes of William Palmer* (1998), starring Keith Allen in the role of the infamous doctor.

The final character to place Rugeley on the map was George Ernest Thompson Edalji (1876 – 1953) who having been educated in Rugeley become a solicitor and was famously, and wrongly, convicted of what was called the 'Great Wyrley Outrages' (i.e. the mysterious mutilation of sheep, horses and cows in the middle of the night in the village of Great Wyrley some eight-and-a-half miles south of Rugeley). He was put on trial, found guilty and sentenced to seven years hard labour. However, he was subsequently cleared chiefly as the result of campaigning by no less than Sir Arthur Conan Doyle, the creator of Sherlock Holmes. Doyle had read about the case in the newspapers and felt compelled to act. To this end he arranged to meet Edalji and saw in an instant that he could not have committed the crimes for as he wrote 'He had come to my hotel by appointment, but I had been delayed, and he was passing the time by reading the paper. I recognised my man by his dark face, so I stood and observed him. He held the paper close to his eyes and rather sideways, proving not only a high degree of myopia, but marked astigmatism. The idea of such a man scouring fields at night and assaulting cattle while avoiding the watching police was ludicrous ... There, in a single physical defect, lay the moral certainty of his innocence'.

SAINT AUGUSTINE'S CHURCH (RUGELEY)

The church of Saint Augustine's, built as a replacement for the original parish church that had become too small, was opened in 1823 by the Bishop of Chester. It stands on land provided by the second Viscount Anson of Shugborough Hall, who later became the First Earl of Lichfield. The building cost £6,501, which was partly met through the sale of materials from the original church, the remains of which are still visible, opposite the current structure. The first vicar of the parish was Henry de Barton in 1276.

The church is of a simple design with pointed windows and other features copying the medieval Gothic style of church building. A new high-quality chancel at the east end of the church consisting of an altar and seats for the clergy and choir was added between 1905 and 1906 at a cost of £4,961, with Lady Alexander Paget laying the foundation stone that contains a time capsule with, among other items, a King George III crown coin retrieved from the foundation stone of the 1823 church. The present chancel with its flanking Lady Chapel, two vestries and organ gallery was designed by Frank L. Pearson. The chancel also includes some splendid stained glass being the work of the well known designer C. E. Kemp, while in the Lady Chapel there is a fine wooden reredos.

As has already been said elsewhere the churchyard is the final resting place of both Christina Collins and John Parsons Cook, who was murdered by Dr. William Palmer (the 'RUGELEY Poisoner').

SANDON LOCK

Sandon Lock (No. 25) is situated on the TRENT & MERSEY CANAL being just over five miles from Great Haywood Junction to the southeast and STONE just under five miles to the northwest. The lock keeper's cottage is a two-bedroom affair and was recently put up for sale by British Waterways with offers in the region of £95,000 being sought. Sandon itself was well known for its lime kiln and mill situated along the canal. At the time Christina Collins passed through the mill was being run for Lord Talbot, after whom the TALBOT INN where Christina's body was taken in RUGELEY was named, for the grinding of Cornwall stone and flint.

SHOULDER OF MUTTON INN (RUGELEY)

Apart from being the place where Thomas Cheshire became drunk this inn also has another claim to fame as it is claimed that the drinking expression, 'What's your poison?' asked when offering to buy someone a drink, originated in this public house often frequented by Dr. Palmer, the 'RUGELEY Poisoner'. It is said that when the rumours were flying around about him having poisoned people he would use the phrase as a joke at his own expense

STAFFORD

Stafford, meaning a ford by a landing place, has a population of over sixty thousand people (and in excess of one-hundred-and-twenty-thousand in the borough) and is of course the county town of Staffordshire, being situated sixteen miles north of Wolverhampton and eighteen miles south of STOKE-ON-TRENT. It is thought that the town was founded in around 700 by a Mercian prince called Bertelin who established a hermitage close to where Saint Bertelin's Church now stands. Indeed by 913 it was the capital of Mercia having been fortified by Queen Ethelfleda, the daughter of Alfred the Great. The presence of clay let to the establishment of the local pottery industry.

In 1069 Eadric the Wild led a rebellion against the Norman conquest resulting in the Battle of Stafford which was largely unsuccessful for in 1070 the Normans built Stafford Castle. By 1206 Stafford had been granted a Royal Charter by King John and became an important market town dealing mainly in cloth and wool. It is said that when King James I visited he was so impressed by the town's Shire Hall he referred to the place as Little London. Stafford, originally a Royalist stronghold fell to the Parliamentarians after a six-week siege, and in 1658 John Bradshaw was elected the Member of Parliament for the town. He is most remembered as the man who judged the trial of King Charles I.

By 1767 Stafford was a centre of shoe manufacture with the largest firm being that of William Horton who through his various contacts, including the famous playwright Richard Sheridan (who was at that time the Member of Parliament for the town), obtained several government contracts. Stafford in the twentieth century became known for heavy industry, in particular electrical engineering.

STAFFORD ASSIZES

The Courts of Assize, or Assizes, were periodic criminal courts held around England and Wales until 1972, when together with the Quarter Sessions they were abolished by the *Courts Act of 1971* and replaced by a single permanent Crown Court. The Assizes heard the most serious cases, which were committed to it by the Quarter Sessions (local county courts held four times a year), while more minor offences were dealt with summarily by Justices of the Peace in petty sessions (also known as Magistrates' Courts).

The word assize refers to the sittings or sessions (from the Old French *assises*) of the judges, known as Justices of Assize, who were judges of the King's Bench Division of the High Court of Justice who travelled across the seven circuits of England and Wales on five commissions namely assize, oyer and terminer, *nisi prius*, peace and gaol delivery, setting up court and summoning juries at the various Assize towns of which STAFFORD was one such location.

It was by the Assize of Clarendon in 1166 that King Henry II established trial by jury by a grand Assize of twelve knights in land disputes, and provided for itinerant justices to set up county courts. Prior to the enactment of *Magna Carta* in 1215, writs of assize had to be tried at Westminster or await trial at the septennial circuit of justices of eyre, but the great charter provided that land disputes should be tried by annual Assizes.

An Act passed in the reign of King Edward I provided that writs summoning juries to Westminster were to appoint a time and place for hearing the causes with the county of origin. Thus they were known as writs of *nisi prius* (from the Latin 'unless before'): the jury would hear the case at Westminster unless the King's justices had assembled a court in the county to deal with the case beforehand. The commission of oyer and terminer, was a general commission to hear and decide cases, while the commission of gaol delivery required the justices to try all prisoners held in the gaols.

Few substantial changes occurred until the nineteenth century when from the 1830s onwards, Wales and the palatine county of Chester, previously served by the Court of Grand Session, were merged into the circuit system. The commissions for London and Middlesex were also replaced with a Central Criminal Court, serving the whole metropolis, and county courts were established around the country to hear many civil cases previously covered by *nisi prius*, and hence the boatmen in the Christina Collins murder had their first trial at the Staffordshire Summer Assizes of July 1839, and being subsequently tried at the Spring Assizes of 1840.

Later the *Judicature Act of 1873* created the Supreme Court of Judicature transferring the jurisdiction of the commissions of assize to the High Court of Justice, and established District Registries of the High Court across the country, further diminishing the civil jurisdiction of the assizes. Finally in 1956 Crown Courts were set up in Liverpool and Manchester, replacing the Assizes and Quarter Sessions, a system that was extended nationwide in 1972 following the recommendations of a royal commission.

STAFFORD COUNTY GAOL

Stafford Gaol, consisting of seven wings, was built on its current site in 1794, and has been in almost continuous use, save for a period between 1916 and 1940. In more recent times the prison has been designated a male category C prison that in November 1998 was heavily criticised by Her Majesty's Chief Inspector of Prisons for lack of security after it emerged that inmates were being supplied with drugs flown in on paper aeroplanes. Inmates were fashioning strips of paper into aeroplanes, then attaching lines to them and flying them over the nineteen feet high perimeter wall. The lines were then used to pull packages containing drugs and other banned substances back over the wall. The prison was also criticised for being overcrowded, under-resourced, and failing to prepare prisoners for release.

In March 2003, the Prison Reform Trust singled out Stafford Gaol for its high turnover of governors (four in five years), but by October 2003 a further report from the Chief Inspector praised improvements at Stafford Gaol saying that it was becoming an effective training prison, specialising in helping vulnerable prisoners and sex offenders.

[No prizes for guessing what is located in this Stafford road]

However, it is the Victorian era that is of most interest here, a time when cells measured either nine feet by eight-and-a-half feet, or seven feet by six feet. All cells were eight-and-a-half feet in height, with there usually being more than one prisoner per cell. Each cell was separated by iron railings allowing prisoners to see each other, and there was a twelve inch square 'trap door' in each cell door to enable warders to check on inmates and to pass meals through. Cell doors were not opened other than at stated times although a prisoner could ring a bell in the case of emergency. A cell consisted of a small table, a metal washing basin, a close closet (introduced in 1882), a small cupboard containing drinking cups, salt cellar, dinner dishes, plates and spoons and in addition there were two brushes issued to each prisoner to keep the floor clean.

Prisoners slept in hammocks, slung from wall to wall, on a coconut fibre mattress, a pair of sheets, two blankets and a rug, with the hammocks being folded away each morning. Each cell had gas lighting and was heated with warm air coming through a filter above the door of the cell.

Upon arrival all prisoners went through a reception area where they were examined by the surgeon. They then had a cold and a hot bath with their clothes being fumigated in an oven and then put into a store room. They were given grey prison clothes with a circular badge for identification to wear, and were afterwards known only as a number from the day of admission to the day of dismissal. Male and female prisoners were kept separate spending their time in their cells except when working, exercising or attending services in the prison chapel. When out of their cells, they were forbidden to talk or wore masks to prevent recognition.

Prison diet consisted of bread and gruel for breakfast and supper, with meat (boiled to make it hard to digest), potatoes, bread, soup and rice for dinner according to the following daily allowances.

Female	per day	Male	per day
Class 5	1 lb Bread	Class 6	1 lb Bread
(4 - 12 months)	1 lb Potatoes	(1 - 3 years)	1 lb Potatoes
	8 oz Oatmeal		10 oz Oatmeal
	8 oz Indian meal		10 oz Indian meal
	1 pint Milk		1 ½ pints Milk

Prison work almost certainly meant the treadmill of which Stafford County Goal boasted eight in 1883. They were large affairs with three of them accommodating two-hundred-and-forty men powering three corn mills as well as a water mill. Prisoners would work nearly five hours a day on the treadmill divided into bells i.e. they worked four bells on with two bells rest taken in the same compartment in which they worked. In addition there was the crank, devised in 1840, which either drew up water or was used for the sake of labour. At Stafford County Goal the cranks were both in the prison cells as well in a shed for men taken off the treadmill and also for cripples. On average the target was fourteen thousand revolutions per day which if not achieved made the prisoner subject to flogging or a missed meal.

The following was the daily routine for the majority of prisoners at this time.

- ❖ 05.45: Bell.
- ❖ 06.00: Prisoners are up, having made their bed or hammock and dressed. Ten prisoners were chosen to draw up water for one hour.
- ❖ 08.00: Breakfast.
- ❖ 09.00: Work.
- ❖ 13.00: Dinner.
- ❖ 14.00: Work.
- ❖ 17.30: Supper. Reading of the Bible, prayer book or other literature approved by the chaplain was allowed. Non-readers were given instruction by the schoolmaster until 19.00.
- ❖ 19.00: Bell. Hammocks down.
- ❖ 19.30: Men and women in bed.
- ❖ 19.50: Gas lights turned out.

STAFFORDSHIRE GAZETTE

Like many provincial newspapers the *Staffordshire Gazette* was for most of its time in financial trouble and subject to takeovers and mergers. It was first published in Newcastle under Lyme on the 6th April 1813, but within a year had become the *Staffordshire Gazette and Newcastle and Pottery Advertiser*. In 1819 it was again renamed as the *Newcastle and Pottery Gazette and Staffordshire Advertiser* perhaps indicating the importance of the Potteries over the county itself. However, although this publication ceased in 1834 another founded by Joshua Drewry, the weekly *Staffordshire Gazette*, ran from July 1831 to September 1832. There then seems to have been a lapse until J. T. Walters in 1838 (1839 in RUGELEY) published a Conservative newspaper by the same name, but this too was to cease in 1842 by which time it was officially called the *Staffordshire Gazette, County Standard and General Commercial Advertiser for the Midland Counties*.

STOKE-ON-TRENT

Stoke-on-Trent, or more commonly just Stoke, is the centre of what is known as the Potteries and became a city in 1925. The name derives from the Old English, *stoc*, which has multiple meanings including dairy farm, secondary or dependent place or farm, summer pasture, crossing place, meeting place and place of worship. It is not certain which of these is the intended meaning, but as might be imagined there were many places called Stoke in the country and hence the affix of the river so as to distinguish it, although over the centuries this has become largely redundant.

Since the seventeenth century the area has been almost exclusively known for its industrial-scale pottery manufacturing with such world-renowned names as Royal Doulton, Spode, Wedgwood and Minton being established here. Allied to this the construction of the TRENT & MERSEY CANAL enabled the import of china clay from Cornwall together with other materials that facilitated the production of creamware and bone china.

The city was until 1994 when the Trentham Superpit was closed the centre of the North Staffordshire coalfield that at its peak gave employment to some twenty thousand inhabitants from the borough. Other employment came from the iron and steel-making industries located at nearby Shelton but this activity ceased in 2002. The fourth industry in Stoke was that of repair shop for the North Staffordshire Railway that operated between 1864 and 1927, and also for the construction of steam locomotives at Kerr Stuart & Co. Ltd. between

1881 and 1930. Finally Stoke was the site chosen in the 1920s by Michelin for their first tyre factory in the United Kingdom.

STONE

Stone is an old market town, of population around fifteen thousand persons, equidistant from both STAFFORD to the south and STOKE-ON-TRENT to the north by some seven miles. The place-name's meaning is exactly what is stated, a 'stone, or rock', from the Old English *stān*. The local story is that the town was named after the pile of stones taken from the River Trent raised on the graves of the two princes, Ruffin and Wulfad, killed in 665 by their father, King Wulfhere of Mercia, because of their conversion to Christianity (after the arrival of that religion via the monks from Lindisfarne to what was then the capital of Mercia). A church was built over these stones in 670 and lasted until the ninth century before being destroyed by invading Danes. It was replaced in 1135 by an Augustinian priory that survived until its dissolution during the reign of King Henry VIII. The building subsequently collapsed in 1749 with the present church of Saint Michael's being built in 1758.

The River Trent runs through the town and has been used for cargo-carrying vessels since Roman times, although passage further inland could only be achieved by small boats. In 1766 James Brindley, the canal builder, put forward a scheme to construct what he called the Grand Trunk Canal to connect the Mersey and Trent rivers. It was backed by Josiah Wedgwood of pottery fame who saw that it offered an efficient way to bring raw materials to his pottery as well as transporting the finished wares to his customers.

By the 29th September 1772 (Brindley having died just two days earlier) forty-eight miles of the Grand Trunk Canal (now the TRENT & MERSEY CANAL) from Wilden Ferry to Stone was navigable. On completion of Star Lock a grand opening was held, and during this ceremony a cannon was fired in celebration. However, disaster struck with the cannon damaging the new lock that was subsequently in need of a re-build! Stone became the headquarters of the canal company with its office at Westbridge House, sited below Star Lock, on what is now Westbridge Park. The offices were later moved to STOKE-ON-TRENT, but at the time of the Christina Collins murder it was to Hugh Cordwell at Westbridge House that she made her complaint regarding the boatmen.

TALBOT INN (RUGELEY)

The Talbot Inn stood at the corner of Anson Street and Wolseley Road. For some of the time between its closure and its demolition it was used as a stores depot for the Army Service Corps, during army manoeuvres on Cannock Chase. It is recorded that there were large manoeuvres in 1873. Apart from that very little is known about the Talbot Inn save that it wasn't perhaps the finest of establishments if the general report of RUGELEY that appeared on the 19th January 1856 (prior to the Dr. Palmer trial) in the *Illustrated London News* is anything to go by:

'An inn in a town is always a representative place. In RUGELEY the inns are as miserably inconvenient, insufficient, and uncomfortable, as posthouse inns in Poland. Like the other houses, they are drear, the principle inn (The Talbot Arms), looks like an aged gaol.'

TRENT & MERSEY CANAL

The Trent & Mersey Canal, consisting of over seventy locks and five tunnels, begins, as you would expect, within a few miles of the River Mersey, near Runcorn, and finishes in a junction with the River Trent in Derbyshire. It is just over ninety miles long and by pleasure cruiser today takes around six days to complete. It is what is termed a minor waterway meaning that for most of its length the bridges and locks can only accommodate a single boat of maximum dimensions seven feet by seventy-two feet.

It is one of the earliest canals, built by James Brindley, with much of historical interest, passing through some pleasant countryside. It struggles from the Cheshire plains up thirty-one locks, often called Heartbreak Hill, to cut beneath Harecastle Hill in a spooky and watery tunnel one-and-three-quarter miles long (HARECASTLE TUNNEL). It passes through the industrial area of the Staffordshire Potteries and out into rural Staffordshire and finally Derbyshire. The first sod was cut by Josiah Wedgwood in July 1766 at Middleport and was opened eleven years later in 1777.

It is of course well documented that the railways were the eventual cause for the decline in traffic on the canals in general, but in the early days of the railways it was the canal owners who were dominant. To stifle opposition to the proposed a new railway between STOKE-ON-TRENT and Liverpool, the Trent & Mersey Canal was purchased in its entirety on 15th January 1847 by the North Staffordshire Railway Company and hence there was consequently no opposition to their plans. However, the line never came into existence due to opposition from other competing railway interests.

[FRADLEY JUNCTION signpost
showing the way to Coventry,
Great Haywood and Shardlow]

In its day the Trent & Mersey Canal was the equivalent of a superhighway being part of Brindley's 'Grand Cross' vision to link the four main rivers in England i.e. Trent, Mersey, Severn and Thames. The northern and eastern arm of the cross were provided by the Trent & Mersey Canal with the central hub being at FRADLEY JUNCTION from where the southern arm to the River Thames started via the COVENTRY CANAL and further along the OXFORD CANAL, with the western arm being the Staffordshire & Worcestershire Canal to the River Severn.

WILLIAM SALT LIBRARY (STAFFORD)

William Salt was born in 1808 in London, the son of John Stevenson Salt and Sarah Stevenson, and the great-grandson of John Stevenson who, in 1737, founded the first bank in STAFFORD. The Stevenson family also established a bank in London, of which William Salt became a partner. By his early twenties Salt had developed an interest in collecting topographical and genealogical books and manuscripts. The financial security from the family business enabled him to pursue this passion throughout his life, and since his family originated in Staffordshire his collections concentrated on that county, however, although during his life he acquired property in Staffordshire he never actually lived there. In 1857 Salt married Helen Black and went to reside at No. 23 Park Square East, near Regent's Park. He died after collapsing on 6th December 1863 and is buried in Highgate cemetery in north London.

He left all his collections to his wife who within five years had had them catalogued and up for sale. This came to the attention of the Lord Lieutenant of Staffordshire and, although Salt's collection of coins, including many Staffordshire tokens and examples from the STAFFORD mint, was sold, Mrs. Salt eventually agreed to donate all his books and manuscripts to the County of Stafford. The resulting library, always called the William Salt Library, was first established in Market Square, STAFFORD, in 1872 moving to its present site in Eastgate Street in 1918. Salt's original collection remains the core of the library although it does continue to add printed books, ephemera, pamphlets and illustrative material relating to the county to act as a research tool for present and future generations.

WOOD END LOCK

Wood End Lock (No. 20) on the TRENT & MERSEY CANAL, between FRADLEY JUNCTION (a mile to the east) and Tuppenhurst aqueduct (two miles to the west), is considered to be a minor waterway feature. It is a single width lock with a rise of just over five feet being of late eighteenth century construction, although the current gates are twentieth century. The lock and bridge, which are grade II listed, are of red brick (English bond) with sandstone arch jambs and parapet coping.

Enjoyed this publication? ... Then you should buy
Inspector Morse on Location ...

From the Greyhound Inn at Aldbury to Wrotham Park in Herfordshire this is the definitive guide to over 60 filming locations outside of central Oxford that are most associated with the *Inspector Morse* and *Lewis* television series. This 80 page book is fully indexed by county, episode and location type and covers everything from pubs and breweries to churches and stately homes. It is fully illustrated and even contains location maps to assist the reader when planning visits.

www.inspector-morse.com
Endeavour House, 170 Woodland Road, Sawston, Cambridge. CB22 3DX

Enjoy *Inspector Morse & Lewis*? ... then join
The Inspector Morse Society

www.inspector-morse.com
Endeavour House, 170 Woodland Road, Sawston, Cambridge. CB22 3DX